A BOOK
CALLED
BOB

A BOOK CALLED BOB

by

SEAN KELLY

WARNER BOOKS

A Warner Communications Company

A BOOK

CALLED

BOB

What do you call a guy with no arms and no legs who's been dropped into the middle of the ocean?

BOB

What do you call a guy with no arms and no legs who's been thrown across the surface of a pond?

SKIP

What do you call a guy with no arms and no legs who's been nailed to the wall?

ART

What do you call a guy with no arms and no legs who's helping to change a tire?

JACK

What do you call a guy with no arms and no legs who's been stuffed into a basket?

DUNC

What do you call a guy with no arms and no legs who gets left behind in a restaurant?

TIP

What do you call a guy with no arms and no legs who has no head?

CHESTER

What do you call a guy with no arms and no legs who has no head and no torso, either?

DICK

What do you call a guy with no arms and no legs who has no head and no torso, but is in disguise?

JOCK

What do you call a guy with no arms and no legs who's been tossed into an Irish fireplace?

PETE

What do you call a guy with no arms and no legs who's always getting dumped on?

JOHN

What do you call a guy with no arms and no legs who's English, and always getting dumped on?

LOU

What do you call a guy with no arms and no legs who's been disinterred?

DOUG

What do you call a guy with no arms and no legs with art nailed to him?

WALLY

What do you call a guy with no arms and no legs who comes in your mailbox once a month?

BILL

What do you call a guy with no arms and no legs who smells like livestock?

BARNEY

What do you call a guy with no arms and no legs in a pot with lots of potatoes?

STU

What do you call a guy with no arms and no legs who falls asleep in front of your door?

MATT

What do you call a guy with no arms and no legs in a nudist colony?

SEYMOUR

What do you call a guy with no arms and no legs flying over the fence?

HOMER

What do you call a guy with no arms and no legs who's covered with mustard?

FRANK

What do you call a guy with no arms and no legs who's covered with sauerkraut?

REUBEN

What do you call a guy with no arms and no legs who's covered with oil?

DEREK

What do you call a guy with no arms and no legs on two wheels?

AXEL

What do you call a guy with no arms and no legs in a motorized wheel chair?

OTTO

What do you call a guy with no arms and no legs with a history of wheelchair collisions?

REX

What do you call a guy with no arms and no legs who fails to catch fire?

DUDLEY

What do you call a guy with no arms and no legs who's upside down in the end zone?

SPIKE

What do you call a guy with no arms and no legs painted with dragons, ships and sunsets?

VAN

What do you call a guy with no arms and no legs with a bad cough?

FLEMING

What do you call a guy with no arms and no legs who's been attacked by tigers?

CLAUDE

What do you call a guy with no arms and no legs who's been run over by a steam roller?

MILES

What do you call a guy with no arms and no legs with rice growing out of him?

PADDY

What do you call a guy with no arms and no legs who's very pale?

ASHLEY

What do you call a guy with no arms and no legs who's Spanish, and very pale?

JUAN

What do you call a guy with no arms and no legs on top of another guy's head?

CAP

What do you call a guy with no arms and no legs on top of a woman's head?

BEAU

What do you call a guy with no arms and no legs of very few words?

KURT

What do you call a guy with no arms and no legs who tastes good?

WINSTON

What do you call a guy with no arms and no legs who tastes like water?

BUD

What do you call a guy with no arms and no legs who tastes even more like water?

MILLER

What do you call a guy with no arms and no legs who's been struck by lightning?

ROD

What do you call a guy with no arms and no legs in Tiffany's window?

JULES

What do you call a guy with no arms and no legs on the president's desk?

VITO

What do you call a guy with no arms and no legs half way down Tina Turner's throat?

MIKE

What do you call a guy with no arms and no legs who's fallen into a bull ring?

GORD

What do you call a guy with no arms and no legs who was left out in a field all night?

DEWEY

What do you call a guy with no arms and no legs who's stealing cattle?

RUSSELL

What do you call a guy with no arms and no legs who makes you an offer you can't refuse?

DON

What do you call a guy with no arms and no legs but who's only pretending to have no arms or legs?

JOSH

What do you call a guy with no arms and no legs who's pretending to have no arms or legs for money?

CON

What do you call a guy with no arms and no legs on drugs?

HY

What do you call a guy with no arms and no legs selling drugs?

RICH

What do you call a guy with no arms and no legs on mediocre drugs?

BUZZ

What do you call a guy with no arms and no legs on Jamaican drugs?

HERB

What do you call a guy with no arms and no legs who's frequently foaming at the mouth?

FITZ

What do you call a guy with no arms and no legs who carries an air horn?

BLAIR

What do you call a guy with no arms and no legs who helps burgle houses?

JIMMY

What do you call a guy with no arms and no legs who has a bullet proof skull?

HELMUT

What do you call a guy with no arms and no legs exposing himself in Saint Patrick Cathedral?

SEAMUS

What do you call a guy with no arms and no legs with a desk job at the precinct?

BOOKER

What do you call a guy with no arms and no legs who's rolling nicely up to the cup?

CHIP

What do you call a black guy with no arms and no legs?

COLE

What do you call a typical guy with no arms and no legs?

NORM

What do you call a Nicaraguan with no arms and no legs?

RED

What do you call a guy with no arms and half legs?

NEIL

What don't you call a guy with no arms and no legs?

1)LEFTY   2)WALKER   3)HANS

What do you call a woman with no arms and no legs who's floating face down in the pool?

FANNIE

What do you call a woman with no arms and no legs who's propped up against the wall?

LENA

What do you call a woman with no arms and no legs propped up against a lamp post?

TRIXIE

What do you call a woman with no arms and no legs caught in a fence?

BARB

What do you call a woman with no arms and no legs on a bun?

PATTI

What do you call a woman with no arms and no legs on bread?

MARGE

What do you call a woman with no arms and no legs hanging in a steeple?

BELLE

What do you call a woman with no arms and no legs every four weeks?

FLO

What do you call a woman with no arms and no legs in the motel room next door?

MONA

What do you call a woman with no arms and no legs with a weak bladder?

PIA

What do you call a woman with no arms and no legs who's been force fed cabbage?

GAIL

What do you call a woman with no arms and no legs with handles?

CARRIE

What do you call a woman with no arms and no legs but who's very popular with the boys?

HEDDY

What do you call a woman with no arms and no legs in a mini skirt?

MAUDE

What do you call a woman with no arms and no legs who has no head and no torso, either?

MUFFIE

What do you call a woman with no arms and no legs who has no head and no torso, either but is in disguise?

KIMBERLY

What do you call a woman with no arms and no legs being pushed across a table?

BETTE

What do you call a woman with no arms and no legs who has an enormous ego?

MIMI

What do you call a woman with no arms and no legs but neatly attired?

NATALIE

What do you call a woman with no arms and no legs at the bottom of an elevator shaft?

DOT

What do you call a girl with no arms and no legs who's been washed ashore?

SANDI

What do you call a girl with no arms and no legs surrounded by hungry truckers?

DINAH

What do you call a woman with no arms and no legs who rolls around on a little cart?

DOLLY

What do you call a woman with no arms and no legs who takes people to court?

SUE

What do you call a girl with no arms and no legs who's invisible?

HEIDI

What do you call a girl with no arms and no legs who's piled high with English produce?

LORI

What do you call a woman with no arms and no legs with a burnt brassiere?

LIBBY

What do you call a woman with no arms and no legs wearing a lamp shade?

TIFFANY

What do you call a woman with no arms and no legs who keeps turning up?

PENNY

What do you call a woman with no arms and no legs with an airfoil on her back?

PORTIA

What do you call a woman with no arms and no legs who's frequently over the counter?

CHER

What do you call a woman with no arms and no legs who didn't know she'd be staying the night?

CONCEPTION

What do you call a woman with no arms and no legs who's totally potted?

FERN

What do you call a woman with no arms and no legs who's a little under par?

BIRDIE

What do you call a woman with no arms and no legs who's been stared at by gypsies?

CRYSTAL

What do you call a woman with no arms and no legs who's being kicked around by Englishmen?

ERIN

What do you call a woman with no arms and no legs on a cannibal isle?

CANDY

What do you call a woman with no arms and no legs and only one eye?

IRIS

What do you call a woman with no arms and half her legs?

DENISE

What do you call a woman with no arms and one leg?

PEG

What do you call a woman with no arms and one leg shorter than the other?

EILEEN

What do you call a Japanese woman with no arms and one leg shorter than the other?

IRENE